Sanjeev Kapoor's KHAZANA Vegetarian Rice, Biryani and Pulao

Sanjeev Kapoor's KHAZANA

Vegetarian Rice, Biryani and Pulao

In association with Alyona Kapoor

www.popularprakashan.com

POPULAR PRAKASHAN PVT. LTD.
301, Mahalaxmi Chambers
22, Bhulabhai Desai Road
Mumbai - 400026

© 2008 Sanjeev Kapoor
First Published 2008

WORLD RIGHTS RESERVED. The contents – all recipes, photographs and drawings are original and copyrighted. No portion of this book shall be reproduced, stored in a retrieval system or transmitted by any means, electronic, mechanical, photocopying, recording or otherwise, without the written permission of the author and the publisher.

While every precaution is taken in the preparation of this book, the publisher and the author assume no responsibility for errors or omissions. Neither is any liability assumed for damages resulting from the use of the information contained herein.

(4072)
ISBN : 978-81-7991-324-6

Design: FourPlus Advertising Pvt. Ltd.
Photography: Bharat Birangi

PRINTED IN INDIA
by Tara Art Printers Pvt. Ltd.
New Delhi - 110002

Published by Ramdas Bhatkal
for Popular Prakashan Pvt. Ltd.
301, Mahalaxmi Chambers
22, Bhulabhai Desai Road
Mumbai - 400026

DEDICATION

To the viewers of Khana Khazana and all my readers who inspire me to create new dishes and rediscover culinary treasures.

AUTHOR'S NOTE

We take rice so much for granted that we rarely give it a second thought. We would look at this indispensible part of our meals in a new light however, if we learned a few interesting facts about this pearly, slender grain.

Rice has been cultivated for over 7,000 years.

There are more than 40,000 varieties of rice.

Rice is grown on every continent of the world except Antartica.

In China, the word for food is the same as the word for rice. The Chinese have a saying, "A meal without rice is like a beautiful woman with only one eye."

The Japanese have a God of rice called Inari; Indonesia has a rice Goddess, Devi Sri.

All over the world, rice symbolises prosperity and fertility.

Though facts about the origin of rice are lost in the mists of time, it is fairly certain that rice was first grown in Asia (either in India or China) and travelled to the far corners of the globe via conquering armies and intrepid travellers. The big name adventurers are all said to have been responsible for the widespread propagation of this humble cereal, from Alexander the Great to Columbus, from the Persians of ancient times to the Portuguese of the more recent past.

While rice is consumed the world over, 90 % of the rice produced is consumed in Asia. The most common form is the simple steamed or boiled rice. More elaborate and exotic dishes have developed over time as local spices and ingredients were added. The humble grain has taken on a luxurious garb, cloaked in aromatic flavours and enriched with among other ingredients, yogurt, butter, legumes, vegetables, meats and seafood. Eastern pilafs, pulaos and biryanis, Creole jambalayas, Spanish paellas, Italian risottos and Egyptian kusheries are all examples of the delectable marriage of rice and a host of ingredients. Closer home, Chitranna, Milagu Jeeragam Saadham, Bhurji Chawar and a myriad regional Indian pulaos and rice dishes are testimony to the versatility of rice.

These are the most common varieties of rice:

Long grain rice includes aromatic varieties like our own Basmati and Patna rice and Thailand's Jasmine rice. The grains stay separate when cooked and are ideal for biryanis and pulaos.

Medium grain rice like Sona Masuri grown in Karnataka and Andhra Pradesh, Arborio which is perfect for risotto and Valencia which gives paella its distinctive flavour.

Short grain rice varieties like the fragrant Ambemohar, which smells of mango blossoms, and sticky Japanese varieties ideal for sushi, are creamy and glutinous when cooked.

White rice is milled and polished rice grains.

Brown rice provides more fibre than white rice as it comprises the bran, husk and germ of the rice grain.

Parboiled rice (ukda chawal) is rice that has been steamed under pressure before it is hulled and processed. It is more nutritious and contains more fibre than milled rice.

Here are some tips for cooking rice to perfection:

- Rinse the rice in several changes of water to remove the excess starch which might make it sticky when cooked.

- For fluffier rice with separate grains, soak it in cold water for at least 15 minutes before cooking.
- Add a little oil to the rice while boiling to keep the grains from sticking to each other.
- Add a little lemon juice for perfect white rice.
- Never stir rice while it cooks – the grains will break, causing the starch to be released, making the rice sticky.
- Cook rice in stock instead of water to add flavour. The general rule is to use twice the volume of liquid as rice.
- You can also get perfect rice by cooking it in plenty of boiling, salted water till tender. Drain the rice, return to the pan and keep covered till ready to serve.
- To test for doneness, pinch a grain. If there is no hard core, the rice is cooked.
- Use leftover rice to make impromptu stir-fries. Just add your favourite spices, cooked vegetables and meats. Make sure the rice is completely cold first.
- To reheat rice, sprinkle with a little water, cover and heat in a microwave oven or over gentle heat.
- For perfect biryanis and pulaos, fry the rice grains till well-coated with fat before adding stock or water.

Happy Cooking!

ACKNOWLEDGEMENTS

- Afsheen Panjwani
- Anand Bhandiwad
- Anil Bhandari
- Anupa Das
- Bhartendu Sharma
- Bharati Anand
- Debashish Mukherjee
- Drs. Meena & Ram Prabhoo
- Gajendra Mule
- Ganesh Pednekar
- Harpal Singh Sokhi
- Jayadeep Chaubal
- Jyotsna & Mayur Dvivedi
- Lohana Khaandaan
- Mahendra Ghanekar
- Manasi Morajkar
- Mrs. Lata Lohana & Capt. K. K. Lohana
- N. K. Krishnanand
- Namrata & Sanjiv Bahl
- Neelima Acharya
- Neena Murdeshwar
- Pooja & Rajeev Kapoor
- Prachi Hatwalne
- Rajeev Matta
- Rita D'Souza
- Rutika Samtani
- Saurabh Mishra
- Smeeta Bhatkal
- Tripta Bhagattjee
- Trupti Kale
- Vinayak Gawande

CONTENTS

Panchranga Pulao	13
Aloo Gobhi Tahiri	16
Matki Bhaat	18
Badi Pulao	20
Ambe Bhaat	22
Bisi Bele Hulianna	23
Chanar Pulao	26
Gorikai Vohre	28
Methi Chaman Biryani	30
Risotto Alla Milanese	34
Kusherie	35
Narangi Pulao	37
Mushroom Dum Biryani	40
Mixed Vegetable Paella	43
Gujarati Khichdi	46
Kathal Ka Pulao	48
Methiwale Chawal	50
Khichuri	52
Bhurji Chawar	54
Chitranna	55
Kumbh Makai Pulao	58
Vaangi Bhaat	60

Sanjeev Kapoor's Khazana

Spring Onion Pulao	62
Kaikari Pulao	64
Ek Handi Nu Dal Bhaat	67
Makhana Pulao	70
Creamy Saffron Risotto	72
Milagu Jeeragam Saadham	74
Handi Biryani	76
Imli Til Ke Chawal	79
Hara Masala Pulao	82
Kathal Ki Biryani	84
Tiffin Tomato Rice	88
Chilli-Mushroom Fried Rice	89
Pudina Paneer Pulao	90
Cajun Rice	92
Dalimbi Narli Bhaat	94
Kaju Moti Pulao	96
Khoya Pulao	98
Herbed Spring Onion Rice	99
Palak Aur Gajar Pulao	100
Thaeer Saadam	103

Vegetarian Rice, Biryani and Pulao

PANCHRANGA PULAO

Ingredients

- 1½ cups Basmati rice, soaked
- 3 tablespoons *ghee*
- 1 inch cinnamon
- 3-4 green cardamoms
- 3-4 cloves
- 7-8 black peppercorns
- 2 bay leaves
- 1 teaspoon cumin seeds
- 2 medium onions, sliced
- 1 medium carrot, diced
- 6-8 French beans, cut into 1-inch pieces
- ½ medium cauliflower, separated into small florets
- ¼ cup shelled green peas
- salt to taste
- 1 medium green capsicum, cut into 1-inch pieces

Rice, Biryani and Pulao — Vegetarian

Method

1. Heat the *ghee* in a thick-bottomed pan; add the cinnamon, cardamoms, cloves, peppercorns, bay leaves and cumin seeds and sauté till fragrant.

2. Add the onions and sauté till translucent. Add the carrot, French beans, cauliflower and green peas and cook for one minute.

3. Add the soaked rice and stir-fry for one minute. Stir in four cups of water and salt to taste. Bring to a boil and cook stirring occasionally over medium heat for three or four minutes, or until all the water has been absorbed.

4. Stir in the capsicum, lower heat and cook, covered, for six to eight minutes, or till the rice and vegetables are cooked.

5. Remove from heat and leave to stand for five minutes. Serve hot.

ALOO GOBHI TAHIRI

Ingredients

- 1½ cups rice, soaked
- 1 medium potato, peeled and cut into ½-inch cubes
- ½ medium cauliflower, separated into small florets
- 2 tablespoons *ghee*
- 1 teaspoon cumin seeds
- 2 bay leaves
- 1 inch cinnamon
- 1 black cardamom
- 3-4 black peppercorns
- 4-5 cloves
- 1 medium onion, finely sliced
- 1 teaspoon turmeric powder
- 1½ teaspoons red chilli powder
- 1 teaspoon *garam masala* powder
- salt to taste

Method

1. Heat the *ghee* in a deep pan; add the cumin seeds, bay leaves, cinnamon, cardamom, peppercorns and cloves and sauté till fragrant. Add the onion and sauté till light brown.

2. Add the potato and cauliflower and sauté over medium heat for two minutes.

3. Add the rice, turmeric powder, chilli powder, *garam masala* powder, salt and three cups of hot water. Cover and cook over low heat for fifteen to twenty minutes, or till the rice is done.

4. Serve hot.

Rice, Biryani and Pulao

Vegetarian

MATKI BHAAT

Ingredients

- 2 cups sprouted brown gram (*matki*)
- 1½ cups Basmati rice
- 2 teaspoons coriander seeds
- 1 teaspoon cumin seeds
- 1 tablespoon grated dried coconut (*khopra*)
- 2 dried red chillies
- 3-4 cloves
- 2 tablespoons oil
- ½ teaspoon mustard seeds
- a pinch of asafoetida (*hing*)
- ¼ teaspoon turmeric powder
- 2 medium onions, chopped
- 2 medium tomatoes, chopped
- salt to taste
- 1 tablespoon grated fresh coconut
- 2 tablespoons chopped fresh coriander leaves

Method

1. Dry-roast the coriander seeds, cumin seeds, dried coconut, red chillies and cloves. Grind to a smooth paste with a little water.

2. Heat the oil in a thick-bottomed pan. Add the mustard seeds and when they begin to splutter, add the asafoetida, turmeric powder and onions and sauté till the onions turn a light brown.

3. Add the ground paste and sauté for two minutes. Add the tomatoes and continue to sauté till the oil separates.

4. Add the rice and mix well. Add three cups of hot water and salt and bring to a boil. Cover and cook over medium heat till half done.

5. Add the sprouted *matki* and mix. Cover and continue to cook over medium heat till completely done.

6. Garnish with grated coconut and coriander leaves and serve hot.

BADI PULAO

Ingredients

- 1 cup Basmati rice, soaked
- 3 (50 grams) *Amritsari urad dal badis*, crushed
- 3 tablespoons *ghee*
- ½ teaspoon turmeric powder
- 1½ teaspoons red chilli powder
- 2 teaspoons coriander powder
- 1 teaspoon roasted cumin powder
- 1 teaspoon *garam masala* powder
- salt to taste
- 4 tablespoons chopped fresh coriander leaves

Method

1. Heat the *ghee* in a pan and sauté *badis* until golden. Add the rice and stir gently.

2. Add the turmeric powder, chilli powder, coriander powder and cumin powder, and sauté for one minute.

3. Add two-and-a-half cups of water and bring to a boil. Lower heat and simmer, covered, for ten minutes.

4. Stir in the *garam masala* powder and salt. Cover the pan and simmer until the water has been absorbed and the rice is cooked.

5. Garnish with coriander leaves and serve hot.

AMBE BHAAT

Ingredients

- 1 cup Basmati rice, soaked
- 1½ medium-sized ripe mangoes, peeled and cut into 1-inch cubes
- ⅓ cup mango purée
- ¾ cup milk
- 2¾ tablespoons sugar
- 2 tablespoons *ghee*
- 1 inch cinnamon
- 2 green cardamoms
- 2 cloves
- 6 almonds, roughly chopped
- 8 cashew nuts, roughly chopped

Method

1. Combine the mango purée, milk, sugar and three-fourth cup of water and stir till the sugar dissolves.

2. Heat the *ghee* in a thick-bottomed pan; add the cinnamon, cardamoms and cloves, and sauté till fragrant.

3. Drain the rice and add to the pan; sauté for one minute. Add the mango mixture and bring to a boil. Lower heat, cover and simmer till the rice is half-cooked.

4. Stir in the mango cubes and nuts. Cover and cook over low heat for another ten to fifteen minutes, or till the rice is done. Serve hot.

BISI BELE HULIANNA

Ingredients

- 1½ cups rice
- ¾ cup split pigeon peas (*arhar dal/ toovar dal*)
- 1½ lemon-sized balls tamarind
- 5 tablespoons oil
- 1 medium onion, sliced
- 3-4 green chillies, slit
- 8-10 *sambhar* onions
- 10-12 curry leaves
- ½ teaspoon turmeric powder
- 3 medium tomatoes, quartered
- a pinch of asafoetida (*hing*)
- ½ teaspoon red chilli powder
- salt to taste
- ½ teaspoon mustard seeds
- 2 dried red chillies
- 4 tablespoons pure *ghee*
- 10-12 cashew nuts

Hulianna Masala

- ¼ cup split Bengal gram (*chana dal*)
- 2 tablespoons split black gram (*dhuli urad dal*)
- 4 green cardamoms
- 4 cloves
- 1 inch cinnamon
- 1 teaspoon fenugreek seeds (*methi dana*)
- 1 teaspoon cumin seeds
- 4 dried red chillies

Method

1 Soak the rice and *dals* separately for twenty minutes and drain. Soak the tamarind in one cup of warm water for half an hour. Extract the pulp, strain and set aside.

2 Dry-roast the ingredients for the Hulianna Masala individually on a *tawa*; mix and grind to a coarse powder.

3 Heat three tablespoons of oil in a pressure cooker and sauté the onion. Add the green chillies, *sambhar* onions, curry leaves and turmeric powder.

4 Add the rice and *dals* with five cups of water and bring to a boil.

5. Stir in the tomatoes, asafoetida, chilli powder, tamarind pulp, salt and Hulianna Masala. Pressure-cook for five minutes.

6. Remove the lid when the pressure has reduced, and stir. If the rice is too dry, add a little warm water.

7. Heat the remaining oil in a small pan; add the mustard seeds and red chillies and sauté till the seeds splutter. Pour the seasoning over the rice.

8. Heat the *ghee* and fry the cashew nuts till light brown and stir into the rice, along with the *ghee*. Mix well and serve hot.

CHEF'S TIP

You can add any vegetables of your choice to Bisi Bele Hulianna. The consistency of this dish should be that of porridge. Use regular rice and not long grain varieties like Basmati.

CHANAR PULAO

Ingredients

- 400 grams cottage cheese (*chana/chenna*), cut into 1-inch cubes
- 1½ cups Basmati rice
- 3 tablespoons *ghee*
- 2 teaspoons sugar
- 1 large onion, finely sliced
- 1 bay leaf
- 1 inch cinnamon
- 2 cloves
- 2 green cardamoms
- salt to taste

Method

1. Wash and drain the rice and spread out to dry. When completely dry, add one tablespoon of *ghee* and the sugar and mix well.

2. Heat one tablespoon of *ghee* in a pan and sauté the cottage cheese cubes. Drain and set aside. Add the remaining *ghee* to the same pan and sauté the onion till crisp and brown. Drain and set aside.

3. To the *ghee* remaining in the pan, add the bay leaf, cinnamon, cloves and cardamoms, and sauté till fragrant. Add the rice and salt and sauté for two or three minutes.

4. Add three cups of hot water and bring to a boil. Lower heat, cover and cook till the rice is done and all the water has been absorbed. Add the cottage cheese cubes and stir lightly to mix. Sprinkle fried onions and serve.

GORIKAI VOHRE

Ingredients

- 1½ cups rice, boiled
- 250 grams cluster beans (*guar phalli*), cut into 2-inch pieces
- 4 tablespoons oil
- ½ teaspoon mustard seeds
- 1 dried red chilli
- ½ teaspoon split Bengal gram (*chana dal*)
- ½ teaspoon split black gram (*dhuli urad dal*)
- a pinch of asafoetida (*hing*)
- 6-8 curry leaves
- salt to taste
- ½ teaspoon sugar
- 1 lemon
- 4 tablespoons grated dried coconut (*khopra*)

Spice Powder

- 2 teaspoons coriander seeds
- 1 teaspoon split Bengal gram (*chana dal*)
- 1 teaspoon split black gram (*dhuli urad dal*)

½ inch cinnamon

1 clove

6 black peppercorns

3 dried red chillies

Method

1. Heat one teaspoon of oil in a pan; lightly roast the ingredients for the spice powder. Cool and pound coarsely.

2. Heat the remaining oil in a pan; add the mustard seeds and when they begin to splutter, add the red chilli, *chana dal*, *dhuli urad dal*, asafoetida and curry leaves.

3. Add the cluster beans, salt to taste and one cup of water. Cover and cook till the beans are cooked and dry.

4. Add the rice and spice powder and toss well to mix. Add the sugar and lemon juice and mix again.

5. Serve hot, garnished with dried coconut.

Note: This spiced rice dish with cluster beans (gorikai) is a speciality of Karnataka.

METHI CHAMAN BIRYANI

Ingredients

- ½ small bunch (75-100 grams) fresh fenugreek leaves (*methi*)
- 300 grams cottage cheese (*paneer*), cut into ½-inch cubes
- 1½ cups Basmati rice, soaked
- 1 cup corn kernels, boiled
- 1½ cups yogurt
- salt to taste
- 1 teaspoon turmeric powder
- 2 tablespoons ginger paste
- 2 tablespoons garlic paste
- 2 green cardamoms
- 1 black cardamom
- 3-4 cloves
- 1 inch cinnamon
- 5-6 black peppercorns
- a generous pinch of saffron
- ½ cup warm milk
- 3 tablespoons *ghee*
- 2 large onions, sliced
- 2 green chillies, chopped

- 2 tablespoons coriander powder
- 1 tablespoon cumin powder
- 1 teaspoon red chilli powder
- 2 teaspoons *garam masala* powder
- 2 tablespoons chopped fresh coriander leaves
- 2 inches ginger, cut into thin strips
- 10-12 fresh mint leaves, roughly torn
- ½ cup fried sliced onions

Method

1 Marinate the *paneer* and corn in a mixture of yogurt, salt, turmeric powder and one tablespoon each of ginger and garlic pastes for about half an hour.

2 Cook the rice in four cups of boiling salted water along with the green cardamoms, black cardamom, cloves, cinnamon and peppercorns till almost cooked. Drain and keep the rice warm.

3 Soak the saffron in the warm milk.

4 Heat two tablespoons of *ghee* in a thick-bottomed pan. Add the onions

Vegetarian

and green chillies and sauté till the onions are light golden brown.

5. Add the remaining ginger and garlic pastes and mix well. Add the *methi* and cook over high heat for ten minutes, stirring continuously. Add the marinated *paneer* and corn. Add the coriander powder, cumin powder and chilli powder and mix thoroughly.

6. Add the salt, half the *garam masala* powder and coriander leaves. Cook for five minutes over medium heat, stirring occasionally.

7. Arrange half the cooked *methi*, corn and *paneer* in a *handi* and spread half the cooked rice on top. Sprinkle some of the remaining *garam masala* powder, half the ginger strips, half the saffron milk and mint leaves.

8. Layer the remaining *methi*, *paneer* and corn mixture on top followed by the cooked rice. Top with the remaining ginger strips, saffron milk, *garam masala* powder and mint leaves.

9. Melt the remaining tablespoon of *ghee* and drizzle it over the top.

10. Cover the *handi* with a lid and seal the edges with dough. Place the *handi* on a heated *tawa* and cook on *dum* for fifteen minutes.

11. Serve, garnished with fried sliced onions and mixed vegetable *raita*.

RISOTTO ALLA MILANESE

Ingredients

- 2 cups arborio rice, soaked for 15 minutes
- 6 cups Vegetable Stock (page 73)
- ½ cup butter
- 2 medium onions, chopped
- 8-10 medium fresh button mushrooms
- 6 tablespoons dry white wine
- salt to taste
- 6 tablespoons grated Parmesan cheese
- ¼ cup cream

Method

1. Bring the stock to a boil and simmer over low heat.

2. Melt half the butter in a heavy-bottomed pan and add the onions. Sauté till they turn a pale pink. Add the mushrooms and rice and sauté for one minute.

3. Add half the hot stock and cook until the rice is translucent. Stir in the wine and salt and cook till the wine has been completely absorbed.

4. Add the remaining hot stock and cook till the rice is tender, but not too soft. Stir in the remaining butter and cheese with a fork. Add the cream and mix well. Serve immediately.

KUSHERIE

Ingredients

- ¾ cup lentils (*masoor dal*), soaked
- 1 cup rice, soaked
- 3 tablespoons olive oil
- 3½ cups hot Vegetable Stock (page 73)
- salt to taste
- ½ teaspoon black pepper powder
- 8-10 garlic cloves, minced
- 1 tablespoon chopped celery
- 2 medium onions, sliced
- 1 medium green capsicum, chopped
- ¾ cup tomato purée
- ¼ cup tomato ketchup
- 1 teaspoon red chilli powder
- ½ teaspoon roasted cumin powder
- ½ tablespoon sugar
- lettuce, to garnish

Method

1 Heat one tablespoon of olive oil in a heavy-bottomed pan. Drain and add the lentils. Sauté over medium heat for five minutes, stirring often. Add two cups

of boiling stock, salt and half the pepper powder. Cook, uncovered, over medium heat for ten minutes.

2. In the meanwhile, make the tomato sauce. Heat two tablespoons of olive oil in a separate pan. Add the garlic, celery and onion and sauté for a while. Stir in the capsicum, tomato purée and tomato ketchup. Add one cup of water, the chilli powder, cumin powder, sugar and salt and cook for three or four minutes over medium heat.

3. Drain the rice and add to the boiling lentils. Adjust stock, cover and simmer over medium heat till both the lentils and rice are done.

4. To serve, arrange lettuce leaves around the edges of a large platter. Place the rice and lentil mixture in the middle, pour the tomato sauce over and serve hot.

Note: This popular Egyptian dish is often topped with crisp deep-fried onions and garlic.

NARANGI PULAO

Ingredients

- 1½ cups rice, soaked
- 6-8 medium oranges
- a few saffron threads
- 1 tablespoon milk
- ¼ cup pure *ghee*
- 2 one-inch sticks cinnamon
- 2 cloves
- 2 green cardamoms
- sea salt to taste
- ¼ cup sugar
- 7-8 black peppercorns, coarsely crushed

Method

1. Cut the oranges in half. Extract the juice and reserve eight halves for serving. Cut the skin (rind) of two oranges into thin strips. Boil the orange rind in water for one minute; drain.

2. Soak the saffron in the milk.

3. Heat the *ghee* in a pan. Add the cinnamon, cloves and cardamoms,

and sauté for one minute. Add the rice and sauté for a while.

4. Add two cups of orange juice and one cup of water. Add the sea salt, sugar, crushed peppercorns and orange rind and stir once.

5. Add the saffron-flavoured milk and stir. Cover tightly and cook over medium heat till done.

6. Serve the rice in the reserved orange halves.

CHEF'S TIP

Cut a very thin slice off the bottom of each orange half to help steady the fruit on the serving dish. Remove the fibres from the insides. Cut the edges in a zigzag pattern for a more decorative appearance.

MUSHROOM DUM BIRYANI

Ingredients

- 15-20 fresh button mushrooms, quartered
- 1½ cups Basmati rice, soaked
- 1 bay leaf
- 4 cloves
- 2 green cardamoms
- 2 black cardamoms
- 1 inch cinnamon
- 1 blade mace (*javitri*)
- salt to taste
- a generous pinch of saffron
- ¼ cup warm milk
- 2 teaspoons oil
- 2 medium onions, finely sliced
- 1 teaspoon fresh ginger paste
- 1 teaspoon fresh garlic paste
- 2 teaspoons red chilli powder
- 1 tablespoon coriander powder
- 10-12 black peppercorns, crushed
- ½ teaspoon roasted cumin powder
- ½ teaspoon turmeric powder

- 2 medium tomatoes, puréed
- ½ cup yogurt, whisked
- ½ teaspoon *garam masala* powder
- ¼ cup chopped fresh coriander leaves
- ¼ cup fresh mint leaves, roughly torn
- 4-5 drops *kewra* water (optional)

Method

1. Bring four cups of water to a boil in a thick-bottomed pan. Add the bay leaf, cloves, green cardamoms, black cardamoms, cinnamon, mace and one teaspoon of salt.

2. When the water starts boiling rapidly, add the drained rice. Cook for eight to ten minutes, or until the rice is three-fourth done, stirring frequently. Drain in a colander.

3. Soak the saffron in the milk.

4. Heat the oil in a non-stick pan; add the sliced onions and sauté over high heat for two or three minutes, or until translucent. Add the ginger paste and garlic paste and sauté for a few seconds.

5. Add the chilli powder, coriander powder, crushed peppercorns, cumin powder and turmeric powder. Sauté for a few seconds and add the puréed tomatoes.

6. Continue cooking over high heat for another two or three minutes, or until the *masala* is fairly thick, stirring continuously.

7. Add the yogurt, *garam masala* powder and half the fresh coriander and mint leaves. Stir well and cook for two minutes longer.

8. Add the mushrooms and salt to taste. Sauté over high heat for two or three minutes and remove from heat.

9. Arrange the cooked rice and mushroom *masala* in alternate layers in an oven proof dish (or *Biryani handi*), sprinkling the remaining chopped fresh coriander and mint leaves, *kewra* water and saffron-flavoured milk over each layer. The final layer should be rice.

10. Cover the assembled *biryani* with a tight-fitting lid and seal the edges with *atta* dough.

11. Place the sealed dish on a medium hot *tawa* and leave for ten to fifteen minutes. You can also place a few burning charcoals on the lid. Alternatively, place the sealed dish in a preheated oven and cook at 200°C for ten to fifteen minutes.

12. Break the dough seal and uncover the dish just before serving.

MIXED VEGETABLE PAELLA

Ingredients

- 1½ cups paella rice (or short grain rice), soaked
- 1 teaspoon butter
- 2 small red capsicums, cut into thin strips
- salt to taste
- ½ cup olive oil
- 1 bay leaf
- 1 medium onion, sliced
- 3 garlic cloves, sliced
- 2 medium tomatoes, chopped
- 1 medium green capsicum, cut into thin strips
- 2 teaspoons paella spice-mix
- a few saffron threads
- 3½ cups Vegetable Stock (page 73)
- 2 vegetable stock cubes, crumbled
- ½ cup shelled green peas, blanched
- 2 lemons, cut into wedges

Method

1. Drain the soaked rice and set aside.

2. Heat the butter in a pan; add the red capsicum, sprinkle salt and sauté for a minute or two. Drain and set aside for garnishing.

3. Heat the olive oil in a paella pan. Add the bay leaf, onion and garlic and sauté till translucent. Add the tomatoes and red and green capsicums and mix.

4. Add the paella spice-mix and saffron and mix well. Add the stock, salt and rice and mix again.

5. Add the stock cubes and half the green peas and cook till the rice is done.

6. Garnish with the remaining green peas and sautéed red capsicum strips.

7. Serve hot with lemon wedges.

Note: Paella spice-mix is a mixture of paprika, which is a mildly spiced chilli powder, and yellow food colour.

GUJARATI KHICHDI

Ingredients

- 1 cup rice (preferably Surti Kolam), soaked
- ½ cup split pigeon peas (*arhar dal/toovar dal*), soaked
- 2 tablespoons *ghee*
- 1 teaspoon cumin seeds
- 2 one-inch sticks cinnamon
- 5 cloves
- 5-6 black peppercorns
- a pinch of asafoetida (*hing*)
- 3 medium onions, sliced
- 2 teaspoons ginger paste
- 2 teaspoons garlic paste
- 3 green chillies, chopped
- 2 medium potatoes, quartered
- salt to taste
- ½ teaspoon turmeric powder
- 3 medium brinjals, quartered

Seasoning

- 2 tablespoons *ghee*
- ½ teaspoon cumin seeds

1 large onion, sliced

4 garlic cloves, chopped

Method

1. Heat two tablespoons of *ghee* in a thick-bottomed pan; add the cumin seeds, cinnamon, cloves and peppercorns and sauté till fragrant.

2. Add the asafoetida and onions and sauté for two minutes. Add the ginger paste, garlic paste and green chillies and sauté for half a minute.

3. Stir in the potatoes and salt. Add the rice, *dal*, turmeric powder and three-and-a-half cups of water and bring to a boil.

4. Cover and cook over medium heat till half done.

5. Stir in the brinjals and continue to cook over low heat till done.

6. For the seasoning, heat the *ghee* in a small pan; add the cumin seeds and sauté till they begin to change colour. Add the onion and garlic and sauté till golden.

7. Pour the fried spices over the cooked *khichdi* and cover immediately. Cook on *dum* for five to ten minutes. Serve hot.

KATHAL KA PULAO

Ingredients

- 1½ cups rice, soaked and drained
- 250 grams peeled unripe jackfruit (*kathal*)
- 2 tablespoons oil
- 2 bay leaves
- 3 black cardamoms
- 2 medium onions, sliced
- 3-4 garlic cloves, crushed
- 1 inch ginger, grated
- 3-4 green chillies, slit
- salt to taste
- ½ teaspoon red chilli powder
- ½ teaspoon turmeric powder
- 1 teaspoon *garam masala* powder
- 2 tablespoons chopped fresh coriander leaves

Method

1. Cut the *kathal* into cubes and deep-fry. Drain and set aside.

2. Heat the oil in a pressure cooker; add the bay leaves and black cardamoms. When they begin to change colour, add

the onions, garlic, ginger and green chillies and sauté till light brown.

4. Add salt, the red chilli powder and turmeric powder. Sauté for a few seconds.

4. Add the *kathal* and stir-fry for one minute; add one cup of water and pressure-cook till the pressure is released twice (two whistles).

5. Remove the lid when the pressure reduces; add the rice and *garam masala* with two-and-a-half cups of water.

6. Bring to a boil and pressure-cook till the pressure is released three times (three whistles). Leave to stand for ten minutes.

7. Remove the lid, sprinkle coriander leaves and serve hot with *raita*.

CHEF'S TIP

Grease your hands and the knife well with oil when cutting jackfruit to prevent the latex in the jackfruit from sticking.

METHIWALE CHAWAL

Ingredients

- 1½ cups rice, soaked and drained
- 1 large bunch (400 grams) fresh fenugreek leaves (*methi*), chopped
- 7 teaspoons oil
- 1½ teaspoons cumin seeds
- 1 medium onion, sliced
- 10 garlic cloves, chopped
- 1 medium tomato, chopped
- 4 dried red chillies, sliced
- 2 teaspoons coriander powder
- salt to taste

Method

1. Heat the oil in a pan; add the cumin seeds and when they begin to change colour, add the onion and garlic and sauté till translucent. Add the fenugreek leaves and sauté for about five minutes.

2. Add the tomato, red chillies and coriander powder and sauté till the tomato softens and the oil separates.

3. Add the rice, salt and four cups of water.

4. Bring to a boil, lower heat and simmer till the rice is done.

5. Serve hot.

KHICHURI

Ingredients

- 1¼ cups rice, soaked and drained
- 1¼ cups split green gram (*dhuli moong dal*), roasted
- ¼ medium cauliflower, separated into florets
- 2 medium potatoes, peeled and diced
- ½ cup shelled green peas
- ½ teaspoon turmeric powder
- 1 teaspoon roasted cumin powder
- ½ teaspoon red chilli powder
- 3-4 green chillies, slit
- salt to taste
- ½ teaspoon sugar

Seasoning

- 8 tablespoons pure *ghee*
- 2-3 dried red chillies
- 1 bay leaf
- 3-4 green cardamoms
- 4-6 cloves
- 1 inch cinnamon

Method

1. Boil eight cups of water in a large pan and cook the *dal* and rice in it.

2. Make a paste of the turmeric powder, cumin powder and chilli powder.

3. Add the *masala* paste, green chillies, cauliflower, potatoes, green peas, salt and one cup of water to the rice and *dal* and cook, covered, over medium heat, for fifteen minutes, or till done.

4. For the seasoning, heat half the *ghee* in a small pan; add the red chillies, bay leaf, cardamoms, cloves and cinnamon and sauté for one minute.

5. Stir the seasoning and sugar into the cooked *khichuri*.

6. Serve hot with the remaining pure *ghee* drizzled on top.

BHURJI CHAWAR

Ingredients

- 1½ cups rice
- 4 tablespoons split Bengal gram (*chana dal*)
- ¼ teaspoon turmeric powder
- salt to taste
- 1 teaspoon *ghee*

Method

1. Soak the rice and *dal* separately for half an hour. Drain.

2. Bring four cups of water to a boil. Add the *dal*, turmeric powder and salt, and cook till the *dal* is tender, but not too soft. Drain and reserve the cooking liquid.

3. Mix the rice with the *dal* and add the cooking liquid and two cups water. Bring to a boil and cook, covered, over low heat till the rice is tender.

4. Drizzle hot *ghee* over the rice and serve.

Note: This simple flavourful rice dish is a favourite in Sindhi homes.

CHITRANNA

Ingredients

- 1½ cups rice, soaked
- salt to taste
- 1 tablespoon oil
- 1 teaspoon mustard seeds
- a pinch of asafoetida (*hing*)
- 6-8 curry leaves
- ½ teaspoon ginger paste
- 1 green chilli, finely chopped
- 2 dried red chillies, broken into bits
- 7-8 cashew nuts, split and lightly fried
- 1 teaspoon split black gram (*dhuli urad dal*)
- 1 teaspoon split Bengal gram (*chana dal*)
- ½ teaspoon turmeric powder
- 2 tablespoons lemon juice
- 2 tablespoons chopped coriander leaves

Method

1. Drain and cook the soaked rice in six cups of boiling, salted water until almost done. Drain and set aside.

2. Heat the oil in a *kadai*; add the mustard seeds. When they begin to splutter, add the asafoetida, curry leaves, ginger paste, green chilli, red chillies, cashew nuts, *dhuli urad dal*, *chana dal* and turmeric powder. Sauté till the *dals* are lightly browned.

3. Add the lemon juice, salt and one tablespoon of water. Simmer for two or three minutes.

4. Add the rice and toss to mix. Cover and cook till the rice is heated through.

5. Serve hot, garnished with coriander leaves.

Note: Whip up this tangy rice dish when in a hurry. It is also ideal for picnics or long journeys.

KUMBH MAKAI PULAO

Ingredients

- 1½ cups, Basmati rice, soaked
- 20-25 fresh button mushrooms, sliced
- ¾ cup sweet corn kernels
- 1 tablespoon oil
- 1 teaspoon cumin seeds
- 1 bay leaf
- 2 cloves
- 5 black peppercorns
- 2 green cardamoms
- 1 black cardamom
- 1 inch cinnamon
- 1 blade mace (*javitri*)
- 1 inch ginger, chopped
- 2-3 green chillies, slit
- salt to taste
- 1 tablespoon lemon juice

Method

1. Heat the oil in a non-stick pan; add the cumin seeds and when they start to change colour, add the bay leaf, cloves, peppercorns, green cardamoms, black cardamom, cinnamon and mace. Sauté for a few seconds.

2. Add the ginger and green chillies and sauté over medium heat for one minute.

3. Add the corn and mushrooms and continue cooking for two or three minutes. Add the rice, stirring gently for about one minute.

4. Add three cups of water and salt to taste and bring to a boil.

5. Cover and cook over medium heat until the water has been absorbed and the rice is cooked. Add the lemon juice and mix gently.

6. Serve hot.

VAANGI BHAAT

Ingredients

- 1½ cups rice
- 5 tablespoons oil
- 8-10 baby brinjals
- 1 tablespoon split Bengal gram (*chana dal*)
- 1 teaspoon mustard seeds
- 6 dried red chillies
- 10-12 curry leaves
- 2 medium onions, sliced
- 4 green chillies, slit
- ½ teaspoon turmeric powder
- a pinch of asafoetida (*hing*)
- salt to taste
- 1½ tablespoons tamarind pulp

Spice Powder
- 15-20 black peppercorns
- 4 dried red chillies
- ½ teaspoon fennel seeds (*saunf*)
- 1 tablespoon poppy seeds (*khuskhus*)
- 2 cloves
- 2 green cardamoms

Method

1. Boil the rice in plenty of water till three-fourth done. Drain well, mix two tablespoons of oil into the rice and set aside to cool.

2. Cut the brinjals into four keeping the stem intact. Soak the *chana dal* for about ten minutes, drain and set aside.

3. Heat two teaspoons of oil and lightly fry the ingredients for the spice powder. Cool and grind to a coarse powder.

4. Heat the remaining oil and add the mustard seeds, whole red chillies, curry leaves and *chana dal*. Sauté till well-roasted and light brown in colour. Add the onions and sauté till pink. Add the green chillies and stir.

5. Add the brinjals and stir-fry over high heat till half-cooked. Sprinkle the turmeric powder, asafoetida and salt. Mix well and add the tamarind pulp.

6. Add the spice powder and cook till the brinjals are almost done.

7. Mix the rice thoroughly into the brinjal mixture and toss over high heat.

8. Lower heat, sprinkle two tablespoons of water, cover and cook till the rice is soft and completely cooked.

SPRING ONION PULAO

Ingredients

- 1½ cups Basmati rice, soaked
- 6 spring onions, sliced
- 3 tablespoons oil
- 1 teaspoon cumin seeds
- 8-10 garlic cloves, sliced
- salt to taste
- 1 teaspoon *garam masala* powder
- 1 tablespoon lemon juice
- 1 cup chopped spring onion greens

Method

1. Heat the oil in a pan and add the cumin seeds. As they begin to change colour, add the spring onions and garlic and sauté until brown.

2. Stir in the rice and mix gently. Add three cups of water, salt and *garam masala* powder and mix. Cover and simmer until the water has been absorbed and the rice is cooked.

3. Sprinkle lemon juice over the rice and serve hot, garnished with spring onion greens.

KAIKARI PULAO

Ingredients

- 1½ cups rice
- 10 tablespoons oil
- 2 medium onions, chopped
- 10-12 curry leaves
- 4 green chillies, slit
- 1 medium tomato, seeded and cubed
- 1 medium green capsicum, cubed
- 1 medium carrot, cubed
- 2 medium potatoes, peeled and cubed
- 10 French beans, cut into ½-inch pieces
- ¼ small cauliflower, separated into small florets
- ¼ cup shelled green peas
- salt to taste
- ¼ cup chopped fresh coriander leaves
- 1 tablespoon lemon juice

Masala Paste

- 10-12 garlic cloves, roughly chopped
- 1 inch ginger, roughly chopped
- ¼ cup grated fresh coconut
- 4 dried red chillies

- 2 tablespoons coriander seeds
- 1 teaspoon cumin seeds
- 1 tablespoon poppy seeds (*khuskhus*)
- 2 tablespoons fennel seeds (*saunf*)
- ½ inch cinnamon
- 2 cloves
- 2 green cardamoms
- 2 blades mace (*javitri*)
- 1 star anise (*chakri phool/badiyan*)
- 10-12 black peppercorns
- a small pinch of nutmeg powder

Method

1. Soak the rice in four cups of water for about half an hour. Drain.

2. Heat four tablespoons of oil; fry all the ingredients for the *masala* paste till light brown. Cool and grind to a smooth paste with a little water.

3. Heat the remaining oil and fry the onions till golden brown. Add the curry leaves, green chillies and *masala* paste. Fry till the oil separates. Add the tomato and cook over high heat till the moisture evaporates.

4. Add all the vegetables and stir. Cook for a couple of minutes over high heat; add the rice with salt to taste.

5. Add three cups of hot water and stir. Bring to a boil over high heat, lower heat to medium, cover and cook, stirring once in a while, till almost done.

6. Stir in the coriander leaves and lemon juice and cover with a tight lid.

7. Uncover the pan when ready to serve.

CHEF'S TIP

Traditionally, Jeeraga Samba rice is used to make this pulao. But you can use any other long grain rice.

EK HANDI NU DAL BHAAT

Ingredients

- ½ cup split pigeon peas (*arhar dal/toovar dal*)
- ¾ cup rice
- 3 tablespoons *ghee*
- ½ teaspoon cumin seeds
- 2-3 cloves
- 4-5 black peppercorns
- 1 bay leaf
- 1 medium onion, sliced
- ¾ teaspoon ginger paste
- ¾ teaspoon garlic paste
- 1 large potato, peeled and cut into 1-inch pieces
- ¼ teaspoon turmeric powder
- ¾ teaspoon red chilli powder
- ¼ teaspoon *garam masala* powder
- 2 green chillies, chopped
- salt to taste
- 1 large tomato, puréed
- 2 tablespoons chopped fresh coriander leaves

Method

1. Heat the *ghee* in a pan; add the cumin seeds, cloves, peppercorns and bay leaf and sauté till fragrant. Add the onion, ginger paste and garlic paste and sauté for one more minute.

2. Add the potato and mix well. Stir in the *dal* and rice.

3. Add the turmeric powder, chilli powder, *garam masala* powder and green chillies and mix well.

4. Add four cups of water and salt. Bring to a boil, lower heat, cover and cook till almost done.

5. Stir in the tomato purée and coriander leaves. Mash the mixture slightly with the back of a ladle.

6. Cook, covered, over low heat for eight to ten minutes and serve.

MAKHANA PULAO

Ingredients

- 1½ cups rice, soaked and drained
- 2 cups puffed lotus seeds (*makhana*)
- salt to taste
- 2 bay leaves
- ¼ teaspoon turmeric powder
- 4 tablespoons *ghee*
- 3 tablespoons oil
- 1 teaspoon cumin seeds
- 2 medium onions, sliced
- 1 cup yogurt, whisked
- ½ teaspoon red chilli powder
- 1 teaspoon *garam masala* powder
- 2 tablespoons chopped fresh coriander leaves

Method

1. Bring six cups of water to a boil; add the rice, salt, bay leaves and turmeric powder. Cook till done and drain.

2. Heat the *ghee* in a pan and fry the *makhana* till light golden and crisp. Drain and set aside.

3. Heat the oil in a separate pan and add the cumin seeds. When they begin to change colour, add the onions and sauté till brown.

4. Add the *makhana* and yogurt and cook till the yogurt begins to bubble; add the chilli powder and salt and sauté till the water has been absorbed.

5. Add the rice and toss well. Sprinkle the *garam masala* powder and serve hot, garnished with coriander leaves.

CREAMY SAFFRON RISOTTO

Ingredients

- 1 cup arborio rice
- a generous pinch of saffron
- 2 tablespoons butter
- ½ large onion, chopped
- 4-5 cups Vegetable Stock (see below)
- salt to taste
- 4 tablespoons grated processed cheese
- ¼ cream
- 1 teaspoon grated Parmesan cheese

Method

1. Soak the saffron in one-fourth cup of warm water and set aside.

2. Heat the butter in a large pan; add the onion and garlic and sauté over medium heat for one minute.

3. Add the rice and sauté till the grains start to swell and burst.

4. Add one cup of vegetable stock, the saffron and salt and stir over low heat until the stock has been absorbed.

5. Add the remaining stock, a few ladlefuls at a time, allowing the rice to absorb all the liquid before adding more, and stirring continuously.

6\. Cook till the rice is tender, but not too soft.

7\. Gently stir in the processed cheese and cream.

8\. Transfer the risotto to a serving plate and serve, garnished with Parmesan cheese.

VEGETABLE STOCK

Place 1 sliced onion, 1 sliced carrot, one 2-3 inch celery stalk, 2 garlic cloves, 1 bay leaf, 5-6 black peppercorns and 2-3 cloves in a pan with 5 cups of water and bring to a boil. Simmer for 15 minutes and strain.

MILAGU JEERAGAM SAADHAM

Ingredients

- 1½ cups rice
- 2 tablespoons *ghee*
- 20-25 black peppercorns
- ¼ teaspoon asafoetida (*hing*)
- 2 tablespoons cumin seeds
- salt to taste
- ¼ teaspoon mustard seeds
- 10-12 curry leaves

Method

1. Cook the rice in four cups of water till just done. Drain and spread on a plate to cool, making sure that the grains do not stick to each other.

2. Heat half a teaspoon *ghee* in a pan; add the peppercorns and asafoetida and sauté over low heat for half a minute. Add the cumin seeds and sauté for half a minute longer. Cool and grind to a coarse powder. Stir the spice powder into the rice.

3. Heat one teaspoon of *ghee* in a small pan; add the mustard seeds. When they begin to splutter, add the curry leaves and remove the pan from heat. Pour the spices over the rice and mix.

4. Add the remaining *ghee* and salt and mix well. Serve at room temperature.

HANDI BIRYANI

Ingredients

- 1½ cups rice, soaked and drained
- 4 medium onions
- a few saffron threads
- a few drops of *kewra* water
- salt to taste
- 2-3 green cardamoms
- 1 black cardamom
- 2-3 cloves
- 1 inch cinnamon
- 1 bay leaf
- 1 medium carrot, cut into ½-inch cubes
- ¼ medium cauliflower, separated into small florets
- 10-15 French beans, cut into ½-inch pieces
- ½ cup shelled green peas
- 2 tablespoons oil + for deep-frying
- ½ teaspoon caraway seeds (*shahi jeera*)
- ½ tablespoon ginger paste
- ½ tablespoon garlic paste

- 4-5 green chillies, chopped
- 1 tablespoon coriander powder
- 1 teaspoon turmeric powder
- 1 teaspoon red chilli powder
- ¾ cup yogurt
- 2 medium tomatoes, chopped
- ½ teaspoon *garam masala* powder
- 2 tablespoons chopped fresh coriander leaves
- 2 tablespoons chopped fresh mint leaves
- 2 tablespoons *ghee*
- 1 inch ginger, cut into thin strips

Method

1. Chop one onion finely and slice the others. Soak the saffron in *kewra* water.

2. Boil the rice in four cups of boiling salted water with the green cardamoms, black cardamom, cloves, cinnamon and bay leaf, until three-fourth done. Drain and set aside.

3. Cook the carrot, cauliflower, French beans and peas in three cups of boiling salted water till three-fourth done. Drain and refresh under running water. Set aside.

4. Heat the oil in a *kadai* and deep-fry the sliced onions till golden brown. Drain on absorbent paper and set aside.

5. Heat two tablespoons of oil in a thick-bottomed pan; add the caraway seeds. When they begin to change colour, add the chopped onions and sauté until golden brown.

6. Add the ginger paste, garlic paste and green chillies and stir. Add the coriander powder, turmeric powder, chilli powder and yogurt and mix well. Add the tomatoes and cook over medium heat till the oil separates. Add the boiled vegetables and salt and mix well.

7. Arrange alternate layers of cooked vegetables and rice in a *handi*. Sprinkle saffron dissolved in *kewra* water, *garam masala* powder, coriander leaves, mint leaves, fried onions ginger strips and *ghee* in between the layers and on top. Make sure that you end with the rice layer, topped with saffron and spices.

8. Cover and seal with aluminum foil or *atta* dough. Place the *handi* on a *tawa* and cook over low heat for twenty minutes.

9. Serve hot with *raita*.

IMLI TIL KE CHAWAL

Ingredients

- 1½ cups Basmati rice, soaked
- 2 tablespoons tamarind pulp
- 3 tablespoons roasted sesame seeds (*til*)
- 3 tablespoons oil + for deep-frying
- 1 medium onion, thinly sliced
- 1 teaspoon ginger paste
- 1 teaspoon garlic paste
- ¼ teaspoon turmeric powder
- 1 teaspoon red chilli powder
- salt to taste
- 2 tablespoons chopped fresh coriander leaves

Method

1. Boil the soaked rice in four cups of water till just done. Drain and set aside.

2. Heat the oil in a *kadai* and deep-fry the sliced onion till golden brown. Drain on absorbent paper and set aside.

3. Heat three tablespoons of oil in a *kadai*; add the ginger paste and garlic paste and stir-fry for one minute.

4. Add the turmeric and chilli powders and stir-fry for one minute.

5. Add the tamarind pulp and cook for two or three minutes. Add salt to taste and mix well.

6. Add the rice and mix thoroughly. Add the roasted sesame seeds and cook for another two minutes.

7. Stir in the chopped coriander leaves and fried onions, and serve immediately.

HARA MASALA PULAO

Ingredients

- 1½ cups Basmati rice, soaked and drained
- 3 tablespoons oil
- 1 inch cinnamon
- 4 cloves
- 3 green cardamoms
- 1 medium onion, thinly sliced
- salt to taste
- 3 cups Vegetable Stock (page 73)

Spice Paste

- 1½ cups chopped fresh coriander leaves
- 8 garlic cloves, chopped
- 2 inches ginger, chopped
- 2 green chillies, chopped

Method

1 Heat the oil in a heavy-bottomed pan; add the cinnamon, cloves and cardamoms. When they begin to change colour, add the onion and sauté till light brown.

2 Add the rice and continue to sauté for five minutes.

3 Add the spice paste and salt and stir-fry for three or four minutes.

4 Add the vegetable stock and bring to a boil. Cook, covered, over low heat till rice is completely cooked.

5 Serve hot.

KATHAL KI BIRYANI

Ingredients

- 1½ cups rice
- ½ kilogram unripe jackfruit (*kathal*)
- salt to taste
- 4 green cardamoms
- 3 black cardamoms
- 3 cloves
- 2 one-inch sticks cinnamon
- oil for deep-frying
- 4 medium onions, thinly sliced
- 3 tablespoons pure *ghee*
- ½ teaspoon caraway seeds (*shahi jeera*)
- 1 tablespoon fresh ginger paste
- 1 tablespoon fresh garlic paste
- 1 teaspoon turmeric powder
- 1 teaspoon roasted cumin powder
- 2 teaspoons coriander powder
- 2 teaspoons red chilli powder
- 3 medium tomatoes, chopped
- 1½ cups yogurt, whisked
- 2 tablespoons chopped fresh coriander leaves
- 5-6 saffron threads

2 tablespoons milk

1 teaspoon *garam masala* powder

10-12 fresh mint leaves, roughly torn

1 tablespoon *kewra* water

Method

1 Soak the rice in three cups of water for half an hour. Drain. Boil the rice in six cups of water, adding a little salt, two green cardamoms, two black cardamoms, the cloves and one stick of cinnamon, till half done. Drain and refresh in cold water and drain again.

2 Grease a knife with oil and cut the jackfruit into slices. Peel and cut into one-and-a-half-inch cubes.

3 Heat the oil in a *kadai* and deep-fry the jackfruit cubes. Drain and set aside. In the same oil, deep-fry half the onions till golden brown and crisp. Drain.

4 In a separate pan, heat three tablespoons of *ghee*. Add the *shahi jeera* and remaining green cardamoms, black cardamom and crushed cinnamon. Add the remaining onions and sauté for a few seconds.

5 Add the ginger paste and garlic paste and continue to sauté. Add the turmeric powder, cumin powder, coriander powder, chilli powder and tomatoes and continue to sauté for two or three minutes. Stir in the fried jackfruit cubes. Add the yogurt, salt and coriander leaves.

6 Soak the saffron in lukewarm milk.

7 Preheat the oven to 200°C.

8 Arrange half the jackfruit mixture in a large ovenproof dish. Spread a layer of rice over the jackfruit. Sprinkle saffron milk, *garam masala* powder, a few mint leaves and a few drops of *kewra* water over the rice. Layer the rest of the jackfruit and rice. Garnish with fried onions, a few mint leaves and remaining *kewra* water.

9 Cover the dish tightly with aluminum foil and cook in the oven for about twenty to twenty-five minutes.

10 Serve hot with *raita*.

TIFFIN TOMATO RICE

Ingredients

- 1½ cups Basmati rice, soaked
- 2 large tomatoes, diced
- 2 tablespoons oil
- 1 inch cinnamon
- 2 cloves
- 2 green cardamoms
- 2 bay leaves
- 1 large onion, sliced thinly
- 1 tablespoon ginger-garlic paste
- ¼ cup tomato ketchup
- ½ cup thick coconut milk
- salt to taste
- 1 teaspoon sugar

Method

1. Tie the cinnamon, cloves, cardamoms and bay leaves in a piece of muslin to make a *potli*.

2. Heat the oil in a pan; add the onions and sauté till light brown. Add the ginger-garlic paste and stir-fry for one minute. Add the drained rice and sauté for five minutes.

3. Add the tomatoes, tomato ketchup, coconut milk and the spice *potli* and cook for five minutes. Add one-and-a-half cups of water, salt and sugar. Bring to a boil, cover and cook over medium heat till the rice is done.

4. Remove the spice *potli* and gently stir the rice with a fork to separate the grains. Serve hot.

CHILLI-MUSHROOM FRIED RICE

Ingredients

- 4 green chillies, finely chopped
- 1½ cups sliced fresh button mushrooms
- 1½ cups cooked rice
- 3 tablespoons oil
- 1 inch ginger, finely chopped
- 6-8 garlic cloves, chopped
- 5-6 spring onions, finely chopped
- a pinch of MSG (optional)
- ½ teaspoon white pepper powder
- salt to taste
- 1 tablespoon soy sauce
- 3-4 spring onion greens, finely chopped

Method

1. Heat the oil in a wok; add the ginger, garlic and green chillies and stir-fry for two minutes.

2. Add the spring onions, mushrooms, MSG, white pepper powder and salt, and stir-fry over high heat for two minutes.

3. Add the rice, soy sauce and spring onion greens. Stir-fry over high heat for three minutes.

4. Serve hot.

PUDINA PANEER PULAO

Ingredients

- 1¾ cups Basmati rice
- ½ cup fresh mint leaves, roughly chopped
- 100 grams cottage cheese (*paneer*), cut into 1-inch cubes
- 2 green chillies, roughly chopped
- 1½ inches ginger, roughly chopped
- ¾ cup yogurt, whisked
- 2 tablespoons *ghee*
- 2 bay leaves
- 4-6 green cardamoms
- 4-6 cloves
- 2-3 black cardamoms
- 8-10 black peppercorns
- salt to taste

Method

1. Soak the rice in three cups of water for half an hour.

2. Grind the mint leaves, green chillies, ginger and yogurt into a smooth chutney.

3. Heat the *ghee* in a thick-bottomed pan. Add the bay leaves, green cardamoms, cloves, black cardamoms and peppercorns. When they begin to sizzle, add the mint chutney and cook for two or three minutes.

4. Add two-and-three-fourth cups of water and bring to a boil. Stir in salt to taste.

5. Add the drained rice and bring to a boil. Cover the pan and cook over low heat for about eight to ten minutes, or till the rice is completely cooked.

6. Gently stir in the *paneer* and serve hot.

CAJUN RICE

Ingredients

- 2 cups cooked rice
- ½ cup kidney beans (*rajma*), soaked, boiled and drained
- 2 tablespoons oil
- 1 large onion, chopped
- 2 medium tomatoes, roughly chopped
- 1 medium green capsicum, chopped
- salt to taste
- 1 tablespoon lemon juice

Cajun Spice Mix

- 1 teaspoon red chilli powder
- 1 teaspoon crushed red chillies
- 2 teaspoons mixed dried herbs

Method

1. Mix together all the ingredients for the Cajun spice mix.
2. Heat the oil in a deep pan; add the onion and sauté till translucent.
3. Add the tomatoes and capsicum and sauté for two minutes. Add the Cajun spice mix and boiled kidney beans and mix well.
4. Stir in the rice, salt and lemon juice. Cook till the rice is heated through. Serve hot.

DALIMBI NARLI BHAAT

Ingredients

- 1 cup rice (preferably *Surti Kolam*), soaked
- ¾ cup field beans (*vaal*)
- ½ cup grated fresh coconut
- 3 tablespoons *ghee*
- 6-8 curry leaves
- 1 medium onion, sliced
- salt to taste
- 1 teaspoon coriander powder
- 1 teaspoon roasted cumin powder
- 1 tablespoon Goda Masala (see below)
- ½ teaspoon red chilli powder
- ¼ teaspoon turmeric powder
- 1 tablespoon grated jaggery
- 2 tablespoons chopped fresh coriander leaves

Method

1. Soak the *vaal* in water overnight, or for at least six hours. Drain and tie in a piece of muslin. Keep in a warm dark place till the beans sprout. Peel before using. (Peeled *vaal* is known as *dalimbi*.)

2. Heat the *ghee* in a thick-bottomed pan; add the curry leaves and sauté till they begin to change colour. Add the sliced onion and sauté for one minute.

3. Add the rice and sauté over low heat for two minutes. Add three cups of water, the *dalimbi* and salt; cover and cook over low heat till half done.

4. Stir in the coriander powder, cumin powder, Goda Masala, chilli powder, turmeric powder and jaggery. Cover and cook till almost done.

5. Add the grated coconut and chopped coriander leaves. Stir, cover and cook for another two minutes. Serve hot.

GODA MASALA

Roast the following ingredients one by one in a little oil. Cool and grind to a fine powder: 1 cup coriander seeds, 2 tablespoons cumin seeds, ¼ cup stone flower (dagad phool), 6 two-inch sticks cinnamon, 16 green cardamoms, 25 cloves, ¾ teaspoon caraway seeds (shahi jeera), 25 black peppercorns, 10-12 bay leaves, 1 teaspoon cobra saffron (nagkeshar), 2 blades mace (javitri), 3 tablespoons grated dried coconut (khopra), 1 teaspoon sesame seeds (til), 3 dried red chillies and 1 teaspoon asafoetida(hing). Makes 100 grams.

KAJU MOTI PULAO

Ingredients

1½ cups Basmati rice, soaked

20-25 cashew nuts

1 cup grated cottage cheese (*paneer*)

salt to taste

3 tablespoons *ghee* + for deep-frying

1 teaspoon cumin seeds

2 black cardamoms

2 cloves

4 black peppercorns

1 teaspoon turmeric powder

Method

1. Boil the soaked rice in four cups of water till just done. Drain.

2. Add salt to the grated *paneer* and shape into small marble-sized balls.

3. Heat the *ghee* in a *kadai* and deep-fry the cashew nuts. Drain. In the same *ghee*, deep-fry the paneer balls till golden. Drain.

4. Heat three tablespoons of *ghee* in a *kadai*; and sauté the spices for one minute. Stir in the rice and salt. Cover and cook till the rice is heated through. Gently mix in the fried paneer balls and cashew nuts. Serve hot.

KHOYA PULAO

Ingredients

- ¾ cup Basmati rice, soaked and drained
- ¼ cup *khoya/mawa*, grated
- ¾ cup sugar
- a few saffron threads
- 2-3 green cardamoms
- 1 tablespoon pure *ghee*
- 4-5 almonds, blanched, peeled and slivered
- 4-5 pistachios, blanched, peeled and slivered

Method

1. Mix the sugar with half a cup of water and bring to a boil. Cook, till the sugar dissolves completely. Remove from heat. Soak the saffron in two tablespoons of water.

2. Bring two cups water to a boil in a pan and add the rice. Cook till the water has been absorbed; stir in the sugar syrup, cardamoms and *ghee*.

3. Mix the grated *khoya* with the saffron and add to the rice. Stir gently and transfer to a serving platter.

4. Garnish with the almonds and pistachios and serve hot.

HERBED SPRING ONION RICE

Ingredients

- 1½ cups brown rice, soaked for 1 hour
- 1 teaspoon dried oregano
- 4 spring onions with greens
- 2 tablespoons olive oil
- 1 teaspoon cumin seeds
- 2 inch celery stalk, chopped
- salt to taste
- 1 teaspoon red chilli flakes

Method

1. Chop the spring onion bulbs and greens, reserving the greens for garnishing.

2. Heat the olive oil in a pan; add the cumin seeds and sauté till they begin to change colour. Add the spring onions and celery and sauté till translucent.

3. Add the drained rice and salt and sauté for one or two minutes. Add four-and-a-half cups of water and bring to a boil. Lower heat, cover and simmer till the rice is almost cooked.

4. Stir in the dried oregano and chilli flakes. Continue to cook till the rice is done. Serve hot, garnished with spring onion greens.

PALAK AUR GAJAR PULAO

Ingredients

- 1½ cups rice, soaked
- 2 medium bunches (400 grams) fresh spinach leaves (*palak*), chopped
- 2 tablespoons oil
- 4 medium carrots, cut into ½-inch cubes
- salt to taste

Masala

- 3 cloves
- 1 inch cinnamon
- 1 teaspoon coriander seeds
- 1 teaspoon cumin seeds
- 1 bay leaf
- 1 large onion, chopped
- 1 inch ginger, chopped
- 10 garlic cloves
- 2 green chillies, chopped

Method

1. For the *masala*, dry-roast the cloves, cinnamon, coriander seeds, cumin seeds and bay leaf for three or four minutes.

2. Grind the roasted spices together with the onion, ginger, garlic, green chillies and one-fourth cup of water to a smooth paste.

3. Heat the oil in a deep pan and sauté the *masala* paste till the oil separates. Add the carrots and sauté for a couple of minutes.

4. Add the soaked rice, salt to taste and three cups of water and stir well. Cover and cook for five minutes. Stir in the spinach leaves.

5. Cover and cook until all the water has been absorbed.

6. Serve hot.

THAEER SAADAM

Ingredients

- 1¼ cups cooled cooked rice
- 5 cups yogurt, whisked
- 4 tablespoons milk
- 4 green chillies, seeded and chopped
- salt to taste
- 2 tablespoons chopped fresh coriander leaves
- 2½ tablespoons oil
- 1 teaspoon split black gram (*dhuli urad dal*)
- ½ teaspoon mustard seeds
- 12-15 curry leaves
- 4 dried red chillies, broken into pieces
- a pinch of asafoetida (*hing*)

Method

1. Combine the rice, yogurt, milk, green chillies and salt in a large bowl.

2. Heat the oil in a pan. Add the split black gram and sauté for half a minute. Add the mustards seeds, curry leaves and red chillies and continue to sauté for half a minute.

3. Add the asafoetida and immediately pour the seasoning over the rice and mix well. Garnish with coriander leaves and serve at room temperature.

New tittles by *Sanjeev Kapoor* From **Popular Prakashan**

My books are not simply a collection of recipes but an attempt to encourage people to cook...and cook with confidence

Chinese Cooking Non-Veg
MRP Rs. 89/-

Chinese Cooking Veg
MRP Rs. 89/-

Veg Recipes from Around the World
MRP Rs. 89/-

Non-Veg Recipes from Around the World
MRP Rs. 89/-

Thai Cooking
MRP Rs. 89/-

Italian Cooking
MRP Rs. 89/-

Microwave Desi Cooking
MRP Rs. 89/-

Traditional Indian Cuisines Punjabi MRP Rs. 89/-

Drinks & Mocktails
MRP Rs. 89/-

Vegetarian Breakfasts
MRP Rs. 89/-

Salads
MRP Rs. 89/-

Street Food
MRP Rs. 89/-

Seafood
MRP Rs. 89/-

Chicken
MRP Rs. 89/-

Desi Mutton
MRP Rs. 89/-

Paneer
MRP Rs. 89/-

Vegetarian Rice, Biryani and Pulao MRP Rs. 89/-

Rice, Biryani and Pulao
MRP Rs. 89/-

JUST RELEASED

Cakes & Bakes
MRP. Rs. 295/-

www.popularprakashan.com

For further enquiries contact:
Popular Prakashan Pvt. Ltd. 301, Mahalaxmi Chambers, 22, Bhulabhai Desai Road, Mumbai 400 026
Phone: 022-23530303 • Fax: 022-23535294 • E-mail: info@popularprakashan.com